MOST ARDENTLY

MELODIES OF LOVE, NATURE, AND DREAMS

JESIYA AHUJA

Made with ♥ on the Notion Press Platform
www.notionpress.com

To Mujarrah and Aashni,

Till the very end, you'll be my very best friends.

Contents

Foreword

In the pages that lie before you, you will embark on a journey through the realms of emotion and imagination. 'Most Ardently' is a collection of poems that encapsulates the essence of human experience—love, longing, beauty, and the mysteries of the natural world.

Within these verses, you will find solace, inspiration, and moments of reflection. Each poem is a delicate brushstroke on the canvas of the heart, inviting you to delve into the depths of your own emotions and connect with the universal themes that bind us all.

From the tranquil gardens where dreams unfold to the moonlit shores where love finds its rhythm, these poems will transport you to places both familiar and unknown. They capture fleeting moments of joy, the bittersweet whispers of memory, and the unspoken desires that lie within us all.

May this collection serve as a reminder of the power of words to evoke emotion and awaken the dormant dreams within our souls. It is my sincerest hope that 'Whispers of the Soul' touches your heart, kindles your imagination, and leaves an indelible mark on your journey through life.

1. STARDUST SERENADE

She has the moon in her heart, that's why stars fall from her lips.
An ethereal girl, will o' the wisps.
The stars come out, just to see her smile.
She walks on galaxies with stars in her eyes.

...

Moon dust in her lungs,
Starlit are her eyes,
She is a child of the cosmos,
A ruler of the skies.

...

In serene melancholy,
Like a rose-nymph.
She heard my wish
upon a star.

2. LUMINESCENCE

You are light. But sometimes you shine so bright I must look

away.

Even so, is it still ok if I stay?

Heaven's in your eyes,

Like petals of light fallen from the sky.

. . .

Your world is the color of pearls;

Pale white and blue and softly glowing.

And your hair on the beach;

Softly flowing.

. . .

So, in a sky full of stars,

He looked,

He looked at her

Like there was something in her

Worth looking at.

3. WHISPERS OF THE FLOWERS

In the pale moonlight,
the flora's scent,
With it's imperial bells
Adorned thy dells,
Comes from far away.

. . .

flower petals for paper,
My love, your love.
I wrote you the sweetest letter,
With love, with love.

. . .

It's been a long time,
We stand far apart,
Your presence still lingers in my dreams.
So over the lilied waters
And in the roses of evening,
I blur into you.

4. SEASONS

Few were my troubles
that january noon,
Like champagned bubbles,
February came soon.

. . .

March was nearly melancholy,
April was full of whispers,
May was full of sighs,
June returned with wimpers.

. . .

July never said goodbye,
The month of august trembled like a butterfly.
A sorrowful september,
Blue cold october,
The last days of november
And December slipped by.

5. HONEYMOON AVENUE

A tiny little cottage
just for me and you,
In a lilac heaven,
On Honeymoon avenue.

. . .

That one fairy night,
pixied dew.
May became june,
On Honeymoon Avenue.

. . .

From our little garden,
A baby dove cooed.
As i watered my plants
On Honeymoon Avenue.

6. BLOSSOMS OF FOREVER

How lovely it sounded,
that delightful little dream,
A place of peace and joy,
A romantic scheme.

...

With lilacs in bloom,
And Pixies in flight,
Our love will be blessed,
On that summer night.

...

And as we tend our garden,
With love and care,
Our bond will only grow
With each passing year.

...

So let's hold hands and walk
Down Honeymoon Avenue,
Where our love will blossom,
Forever anew.

7. BITTERSWEET BUBBLES

You won't remember,
all my champagne troubles,
But as we sip, those problems arise,
Little things that we can't disguise,
Bittersweet were the bubbles.

...

The bottle won't open, the cork is stuck tight,
Our laughter fades, our mood takes a slight.
We struggle and strain, but can't seem to cope,
These little champagne problems are testing our hope.

...

Champagne troubles, so bittersweet,
As she walked away with heavy feet,
Her heart shattered, but still beating strong,
For one day, she'll find love where she belongs.

8. YOU AND I

Wrapped in warmth,
And you're sealed with safety,
Everything is perfectly fine.

. . .

As I walked along the aisle,
I filled my basket,
I bought you your clementines.

. . .

While outside it rains
We hide in bed,
Just me and you and I.

9. BOMBAY TO GOA

From Bombay to Goa, my heart did roam,
In search of love, a place to call home.
But every road led me back to the sea,
Where the waves whispered of what could never be.

. . .

Dinner at 8 was our plan for the night,
We dressed up nice, and everything felt right.
But as the hours passed, you never showed,
And my hopes and dreams were cruelly towed.

. . .

The emptiness I feel is hard to bear,
As I sit here alone, with nothing to share.
The memories we made, seem so far,
And my heart aches for the way things are.

. . .

From Bombay to Goa, our dreams were bright,
But now they're shattered in the night.
I miss you more than words can say,
As I sit alone at dinner at 8.

10. TANGERINES

Tangerines in hand, I think of school,
We act stupid and laugh like fools,
As the seventh period rolls around,
The tangerines in my bag are nowhere to be found.

. . .

We'd peel the fruit and share a slice,
The sweet and sour taste so nice,
Juice dripped down our chins,
As we giggled and grinned.

. . .

Those moments may seem small,
But they meant the world to us all,
For in those moments we found joy,
A treasure that nothing could destroy.

. . .

And though it's passed, the memory lingers,
In the sweet aroma of tangerine fingers,
A reminder that even the smallest things,
Can hold significance and memories that cling.

. . .

I hold tangerines close to my heart,
And remember those days, never to depart,

For that memory lives on in every fruit,
And in every moment, cherished and acute.

• 11 •

11. SHORES OF BLISS

The sand on our knees and the sun in our sheets,
Memories of summer that our heart still keeps,
The salty air and the crashing waves,
Our carefree days, our youthful ways.

...

We ran along the shoreline with the sand in our toes,
Our laughter echoing, our happiness glows,
The sun kissed our skin with its warm embrace,
And time stood still in that perfect place.

...

We built sandcastles and collected seashells,
Watched seagulls soar and listened to ocean swells,
We danced in the water and felt so alive,
With the world at our feet and our dreams to thrive.

...

The ocean stretched out before us in shades of blue,
A vast and endless horizon, so serene and true,
We watched as seagulls soared above,
And felt the freedom of a life lived in love.

...

And though time may pass, and seasons change,
The memories of that summer will forever remain,

A treasure in our hearts, a source of light,
A reminder of a time when everything felt just right.

12. POMEGRANATE STAINS

Pomegranate stains upon my dress,
A juicy reminder of sweetness,
The burst of flavor in my mouth,
A momentary bliss, nothing less.

. . .

The ruby red seeds, so many,
Remind me of life's possibilities,
Each one bursting with potential,
A universe within a fruit, unbelievable.

. . .

And yet, with each seed that falls,
A stain upon my dress, it calls,
Of the messiness of life's journey,
Of the beauty in the imperfect and blurry.

. . .

For even as I try to clean,
The stain remains, a mark, unseen,
But it reminds me of the taste,
Of the joy that I must not waste.

. . .

So I wear my dress with pride,
With pomegranate stains, side by side,
For they remind me of life's essence,
And all the beauty in its presence.

13. LOVE'S CELESTIAL TAPESTRY

I am in love with the ocean
And the waves that crash and roar,
The way they ebb and flow
On the sandy shore.

. . .

I am in love with the moon
And all the stars up high,
The way they shine and sparkle
In the vast and endless sky.

. . .

I am in love with the flowers
And the way they bloom and grow,
The way they sway and dance
In the gentle breeze that blows.

. . .

But most of all, I am in love
With you, my dearest one,
The way you light up my world

Like the morning sun.

. . .

You are my shining star,
My ocean breeze, my flower fair,
The one who brings me joy
And shows me how to care.

. . .

So let us dance together
Underneath the moonlit sky,
And be forever in love
Until the end of time.

14. FADED FRAGRANCE

An empty bottle of perfume,
A remnant of a scent now gone,
It once held fragrant memories,
But now its purpose seems undone.

. . .

Once it adorned a dresser top,
A symbol of beauty and grace,
But now it sits forgotten,
In a corner, out of place.

. . .

But perhaps this empty vessel,
Can still hold meaning and worth,
As a reminder of past pleasures,
And the memories it gave birth.

. . .

For even though its fragrance fades,
And its purpose may seem lost,
It still holds the power to evoke,
The memories that came at a cost.

. . .

Empty perfume bottles I treasure,
As emblems of love and bliss,
And let the memories they embody endure,
Despite time's relentless abyss.

15. BOUDOIR SLIPPERS

In boudoir slippers, she glides with grace,
A scent of French perfume trailing in her wake.
Silken fabric sways with each gentle pace,
As she moves with the elegance of a queenly race.

. . .

Her boudoir slippers, a delicate hue,
Pink as a rosebud, soft as a morning dew.
And her French perfume, a fragrance divine,
Whispering secrets of a life so refined.

. . .

She dances alone in the dim candlelight,
Her boudoir slippers tapping to a rhythm that's light.
Her French perfume filling the air,
As she loses herself in the moment, without a care.

. . .

Oh, how she sparkles, like a star in the night,
where her boudoir slippers and her French perfume are right.
She lives in a world of beauty and art,
Where every movement is a work of her heart.

. . .

In boudoir slippers and French perfume,
She's the epitome of glamour in the room.
And as she twirls and sways with such grace,
She leaves a trail of elegance in her place.

16. SECRET DOOR

Going for dreamy walks in the afternoon,
taking in the neighbourhood trees and birdsong,
But here i lie in my room,
Rotting away where I belong.

. . .

Flowy, billowy blouses i'd pair,
With dainty flowers adorning my hair.
But here i lay,
From january to may
With my wornout clothes on display.

. . .

Cherry blossom petals would fall,
With pink forget me nots and white bluebells,
I'm on the edge, i might fall,
I hear the ring of the door bell.

. . .

I finally get up from this hell hole
my feet hit the blue cold floor,
And there i find,
The secret garden's secret door.

17. SECRET GARDEN

In twilight's hush, where whispers stray,
There lies a realm where dreams hold sway.
A tapestry of mystic lore,
Where secrets dwell and shadows pour.

. . .

Beyond the veil of verdant sheen,
A hidden place, serene, unseen,
There blooms a garden, bathed in light,
A haven born from day and night.

. . .

Within its gates, a symphony,
Of fragrant blooms and melodies.
Each petal's kiss, a soft caress,
A tender dance, in nature's dress.

. . .

Oh, secret garden, realm of grace,
Where miracles find their sacred space.
With every step, a new delight,
As wonder weaves its purest flight.

. . .

Through ivy archways, whispers flow,
The language known to souls who know.

MOST ARDENTLY

The robin's song, a joyful hum,
The language spoken, heart to heart, sung.

. . .

With gentle hands, the earth's embrace,
Awakens life, a sacred chase.
The gardener's touch, a healing balm,
Reviving spirits, bringing calm.

. . .

Beneath the moon's enchanting spell,
A story whispers, weaves its spell.
A key, a door, a child's quest,
To find the secrets that lie abreast.

. . .

In friendships forged, hearts intertwined,
The healing power of love, refined.
As souls awaken, darkness fades,
And sunlight bathes the secret glades.

. . .

Oh, secret garden, refuge rare,
Where hope blossoms, banishing despair.
A sanctuary for hearts untamed,
A sanctuary where dreams are named.

. . .

So let's wander, you and I,
Beneath the azure, endless sky.
Embrace the wonders yet unseen,
In the secret garden, forever green.

18. KOI POND

In a tranquil garden, where whispers reside,
Beneath a tender moon, love's dance applied,
A koi pond gleams, with secrets untold,
Reflecting the tale of a love so bold.

...

Your dimples are my angels' kisses,
Embracing my heart with tender blisses,
Each curve and contour, a celestial art,
Guiding my soul to its core, to its start.

...

Within this sanctuary, where passions entwine,
We navigate the currents, our hearts intertwine,
Your river flowed gently, a serenade so sweet,
Melting my worries, laying them at your feet.

...

As the breeze blew intently, a delicate caress,
Whispering love's verses, so tender, no less,
In its gentle whispers, our dreams took flight,
A symphony of love, painting the starry night.

...

The koi swim gracefully, in their watery abode,
With colors vibrant, like our love's untold,

Teeming with my fishes, like thoughts of you,
In this pond of devotion, our love is true.

. . .

For with each passing ripple, our love expands,
Two souls forever entwined, held by hands,
In this realm of tranquility, where time stands still,
Our love blossoms, an eternal thrill.

. . .

Your dimples are my angels' kisses,
Your river flowed gently, as passion insists,
As the breeze blew intently, our love it enlivens,
In this koi pond of love, forever we're smitten.

19. SOFT KITTY WARM KITTY

In the realm of dreams, where slumber reigns,
Where thoughts take flight and release their chains,
I find solace and peace, a refuge so true,
Where I rest like a kitten, fresh as a daisy anew.

. . .

As the night unveils its celestial curtain,
And the stars twinkle, their radiance uncertain,
I lay down my worries, my burdens at bay,
And surrender to sleep's gentle sway.

. . .

Oh, to sleep like a kitten, so soft and serene,
Curled up in warmth, where tranquility convenes,
In dreams, I wander through ethereal meadows,
Where fragrant blossoms bloom, their beauty bestows.

. . .

Through the fields of slumber, I frolic and play,
With the grace of a kitten, nimble and gay,
My spirit unburdened, my heart light as air,
In this sanctuary of dreams, I find solace rare.

. . .

Fresh as a daisy, I wake from my repose,
Gently opening my eyes as the morning light flows,
The cares of the world seem distant, so far,
For in sleep's sweet embrace, I've found a star.

. . .

So let the night embrace you, dear friend,
Where sleep like a kitten, with dreams to attend,
Awaken refreshed, like a daisy in bloom,
With a heart full of joy, dispelling all gloom.

. . .

For in the realm of dreams, we find respite,
A haven of serenity, where worries take flight,
Sleep like a kitten, fresh as a daisy's bloom,
And let your spirit soar, unfettered, unassuming.

20. MOST ARDENTLY

In the realm where dreams do dwell,
Where sunsets paint the sky so well,
I weave a tapestry of words,
To capture moments yet unheard.

. . .

Through the meadows, soft and green,
Where whispers of love are often seen,
I wander with a heart so true,
To find a love that's meant for two.

. . .

The moonlight dances on the stream,
While stars above their secrets gleam,
I seek a love that's pure and free,
A love that's bound by destiny.

. . .

With every step, my hope expands,
As fate aligns its guiding hands,
For in this quest, my soul is bent,
To find the love that's heaven-sent.

. . .

With every breath, I search and seek,
Through mountains high and valleys deep,

MOST ARDENTLY

To find a love that will ignite,
A flame that burns both day and night.

. . .

And when at last our paths align,
Your hand in mine, our souls entwined,
I'll hold you close, my heart content,
With a love that's infinite, heaven-sent.

. . .

For in this love, so pure and true,
I'll cherish every moment with you,
And as we journey, hand in hand,
I'll love you most ardently, my love, I stand.

Most Ardently, Jesiya

www.ingramcontent.com/pod-product-compliance
Lightning Source LLC
Chambersburg PA
CBHW020519160726
47991CB00007B/3022